EXCEL PIVOT TABLES And PIVOT CHARTS NINJA

HENRY E. MEJIA

EXCEL PIVOT TABLES AND PIVOT CHARTS NINJA

Copyright © 2021 HENRY E. MEJIA

All rights reserved. No part of this publication may be reproduced, stored in any data retrieval system or transmitted in any form or by any electronic, mechanical, photocopying, recording or other means, without the prior written permission of the author, except in the case of brief reviews used in literary reviews and certain non-commercial uses provided by the Copyright Law.

DEDICATION

To my parents, who have taught me that life is about overcoming obstacles and enjoying it.

CONTENTS

	Introduction	3
	Get your 40 practice spreadsheets	6
1	The Creative Process	8
2	Databases	12
3	Pivot Table Creator	17
4	Pivot Tables With 2 Variables	30
5	Pivot Tables With 3 Variables	42
6	"Summarize By"	51
7	"Show Data As"	59
8	Slicers (Advanced Filters)	74
9	Pivot Charts	91
10	Dynamic Pivot Charts Using Slicers	102
11	Quick Final Tips	117
	I Would Love to Know Your Comments	127

ACKNOWLEDGMENTS

I would like to thank all those who supported me throughout the creation of this book, either with words of encouragement or ideas for this book.

INTRODUCTION

Welcome to a new EXCEL NINJA book! The fastest, the most practice-based and definitely the most straightforward Excel Book Series you will ever find!

You will learn to use with outstanding confidence PIVOT TABLES as well as PIVOT CHARTS!

Excel Ninja Series is all about this:

- **Learning fast**
- **Having fun while learning**
- **Learning trough practice (from the very beginning)**
- **No unnecessary fillers to make the book look longer**

- **The most straightforward and lean approach**
- **Getting results!**

Loaded with a gigantic amount of practice spreadsheets, examples, and recommendations.

My goal for this Excel Ninja Series was to achieve the perfect balance between a lot of exercises and examples without compromising the straightforward approach, and that's what you will find here!

That being said, I would like to summarize the benefits of becoming an Excel PIVOT TABLES and PIVOT CHARTS Ninja:

- Increased chances of getting a promotion and better jobs (Because you are more productive and have better skills)
- Less workload (Excel does the heavy lifting)
- More free time

- Less stress
- A sense of growth (When you learn something new you feel great, and you know it!)
- Etc., etc.

I could spend more time, word and pages explaining to you the benefits and the importance of becoming an EXCEL PIVOT TABLES and PIVOT CHARTS NINJA, but I promised that I won't fill this book with unnecessary words so let's start the first chapter right now!

GET YOUR 40 PRACTICE SPREADSHEETS (.XLSX)

Before starting Chapter 1 I recommend you to get your 40 practice spreadsheets. Those exercise files are included for everyone who purchases this book. They will serve you at the end of each chapter to reinforce what you have learned and make sure you have learned it well.

To get them immediately just **Scan this QR Code** or go directly to **https://bit.ly/hemejia2** and follow the instructions.

If for any reason both the QR Code and the Link don't work, send an email to ems.online.empire@gmail.com saying:

"Hello, I bought your book PIVOT TABLES & PIVOT CHARTS NINJA and I need the 40 practice spreadsheets"

I will gladly reply to you but you may need to wait a few business days.

Now you are ready to start Chapter 1. Let's go!

CHAPTER 1:

THE CREATIVE PROCESS

This book is one of my favorite because it blends 2 of the most important features in Excel: Pivot Tables and Charts.

Because Regular Charts are static and Pivot Tables are dynamic and flexible, instead of using regular charts we need to use Pivot Charts (more on this later)

Regarding the title of this chapter, by creative process I don't mean "innovative" but the process to "create" the desired outcome, which is, a great Pivot Chart that conveys what you want to convey exactly. Thus, following this process is science and art.

It is science because you'll need some specific steps and rules to follow through, nevertheless you'll also have the ability to move away from the rule to create your own Pivot Tables and Pivot Chart.

SO, WHAT IS THE CREATIVE PROCESS?

Is the process by which you take Raw data from a DATABASE and convert that in to a PIVOT TABLE, then you create a CHART (PIVOT CHART) attached to that PIVOT TABLE, and at the end you add some filters in form of SLICERS to create a DYNAMIC PIVOT TABLE thus, creating a DYNAMIC PIVOT CHART also.

Confused enough? Let's what a diagram to better understand this

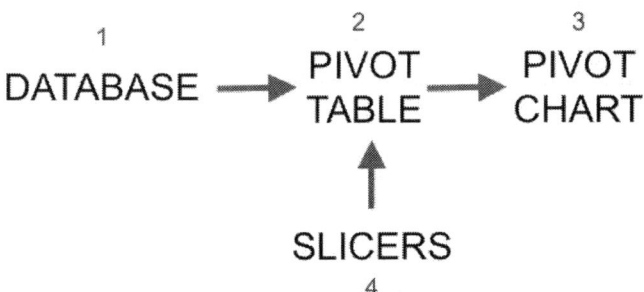

As you may see, having an organized database is the first phase. Without one good database we are screwed.

Then, the second phase is to create the Pivot Table with the data from the data base. You need to create the correct pivot table that serves to your purpose because, as you will learn later in this book, you will have hundreds of variants to create your pivot table.

Third, when you have your Pivot Table in place is the time to attach the suitable chart to it. Why the suitable chart? Because You need the right one to Show the right message.

Last but not least, we'll add movement and flexibility to your chart creating the correct slicers.

And that, boys and girls, is the Creative Process.

QUICK CHAPTER SUMMARY

- The Creative Process has 4 phases
- Each phase needs to be built before you move to the next phase
- This is one of my favorite books!

CHAPTER 2:

DATABASES

Databases are the very beginning of our journey, so it is important that we define what a Database is:

A Database is a complete set of Raw Data, organized in Rows and Columns, containing all the information you need to analyze in order to make decisions.

So, in simple words, it is a spreadsheet packed with data! Normally, that data is created with each transaction that is made, as an example, each sale, each purchase, each expenditure.

If you want to put it in another way, Databases are the raw material that feeds your

Pivot Table.

Just look at this database, then imagine that it has 500 transactions (500 rows)

REALTOR	BUYER	TRANSACTION PRICE	TYPE	CATEGORY
Doctor Strange	Dragon Real Estate Company	$ 506,737	OFFICE	COMMERCIAL
Jiraiya	Marvell Real Estate Holding	$ 924,037	HOUSE	RESIDENTIAL
Wonder Woman	Justice League REIT	$ 1,092,332	APARTMENT	RESIDENTIAL
Ant-Man	Star Realtors Inc	$ 831,484	CONDO	RESIDENTIAL
Indiana Jones	Justice League REIT	$ 992,182	DUPLEX	RESIDENTIAL
Gohan	Lord of The Real Estate Inc	$ 1,401,112	STORE	COMMERCIAL
Storm	Dragon Real Estate Company	$ 741,725	OFFICE	COMMERCIAL

So, in order for you to "get the right answers" to your questions FAST, you will need to create a Pivot Table out of this Database.

In order to value something, we need to know what happens when we are not allowed to use it. So, let's start with some simple exercises for you to know the power of Pivot Tables by NOT using them.

Open file PivotNinjaChapter2ex1.xlsx

You'll notice it is a Real Estate Transactions Database, and indeed, you have almost 550 transactions there.

I'm going to ask you to answer the following questions WITHOUT using Pivot Tables. If you want to use some filters, use them, it is ok.

INSTRUCTIONS

1. Find the answer to every question
2. Measure how much time you are using to answer each one of the questions and write i

QUESTIONS:

- Find the total amount of sales (transaction price) made by Ron Weasley

- Find the total amount of money paid (transaction price) by Dragon Real Estate Company
- How much commission did Iron Man and Captain America made together by selling Residential properties?
- How much incoming Cashflow are Justice League REIT and Star Realtors Inc getting from Downtown properties?
- Which Realtor is the best at selling Offices?

That's it! Please write the amount of time you used to answer each question.

Now, notice the following bold statements I'm making:

When you become a Pivot Table Ninja, you are able to answer ALL OF THEM in less than 2 minutes!

When you become a Pivot Charts Ninja, you are able to put those answers in visual representations AND change those visual

representation **WITHIN SECONDS** in case you need to answer another question!

So, in the following chapters you are going to learn how to answer all of these questions FAST and EASILY. Moreover, you are going to learn to answer any question that can be answered with the Raw Data from the Database!

Let's go to the next chapter.

QUICK CHAPTER SUMMARY:

- Databases are a set of raw Data
- Databases feed your Pivot Tables and then you Pivot Tables feed your Pivot Charts
- Answering questions (regarding a Database) without Pivot Tables is suicidal

CHAPTER 3:

PIVOT TABLE CREATOR

So, the Pivot Table Creator is the MAIN PART OF A PIVOT TABLE. Almost everything that you want to create or modify in your Pivot Table must be done here.

Unlike regular Excel Tables or Databases, Pivot Tables are shaped without touching the Pivot Table itself. That is what the Pivot Table Creator is for, to shape your Pivot Table the way you want and to give it an enormous flexibility.

The Pivot Table Creator looks like this (More on how to use it in the next chapter):

PIVOT TABLE FIELDS

First, you have the Pivot Table Fields and if you put enough attention, those fields are the Top each one of the Columns in the previous exercise.

Open the spreadsheet from the last Chapter and you'll notice that the Database have 8 columns, and those columns are labeled the same as the Pivot Table Fields.

Those fields appear automatically when you pick a Database to work with in order to create a Pivot Table. So, I ordered excel to create a Pivot Table with the Real Estate Database and all I got was the Pivot Table Creator with those fields (more on how to do that step in the next chapter).

To summarize, the Pivot Table Fields are the Columns in your Database.

FILTERS

In a similar way to the Filters in a regular table, you can add some filters to your Pivot Table in order for it to change when you select different items.

Nevertheless, I find filters a little bit annoying and I rather use SLICERS, which are an enhanced form of filters (More on

Slicers later in the book)

To summarize filters, I have to say that Pivot Tables alone allow to filter information to get great answers, but filters allow an even deeper customization of the information presented. Nevertheless, I prefer to create Slicers instead of filters.

ROWS

Now, Rows are mandatory when you are creating a Pivot Table. When you drag a Field into the Row space, what you are ordering Excel is to use the data of that Field and display it as the Rows in the Pivot Table. The Field you choose determines how many rows will appear.

Take as an example the field BUYER in the Pivot Table Fields. Remember that, in the Database, you have some BUYERS there, so if you choose that as the ROWS, you will see all of them (Dragon Real State, Justice League REIT, Star Realtors Inc, etc) listed in the Rows automatically.

	COLUMN
ROW	$
ROW	$
ROW	$
ROW	$
ROW	$

After doing that, you have one piece of your Pivot Table, but it is still incomplete.

COLUMNS

Columns, just as rows, will also appear in your Pivot Table. The Field you choose y determines how many columns the Pivot Table will have.

Taking the previous example, you had BUYERS in the Row section, and if you choose **CATEGORY** as the Column Section you will have 2 columns displayed: **RESIDENTIAL and COMMERCIAL.**

	RESIDENTIAL	**COMMERCIAL**
BUYER	$	$
BUYER	$	$
BUYER	$	$
BUYER	$	$
BUYER	$	$

So, fast and automatically you can get some info **divided by BUYER and CATEGORY.**

I you had chosen **TYPE** as Columns you would have gotten something like this.

	APARTMENT	OFFICE	STORE	DUPLEX	HOUSE
BUYER	$	$	$	$	$
BUYER	$	$	$	$	$
BUYER	$	$	$	$	$
BUYER	$	$	$	$	$
BUYER	$	$	$	$	$

Why? Because the TYPE field has all of those different data inside the Database.

VALUE

At the end of the Pivot Table creation, you will have to decide WHICH VALUE you want to know. Do you want to know the Transaction amount? Do you want to know the total Cashflow? Do you want to know how many transactions were made?

Let's say that you want to know the Transaction amount (in dollars). So, you would pick TRANSACTION PRICE field and use it in the Value Section. Then, you will have your Pivot Table completed.

	APARTMENT	OFFICE	STORE	DUPLEX	HOUSE
BUYER	$$$$$$	$$$$$$	$$$$$$	$$$$$$	$$$$$$
BUYER	$$$$$$	$$$$$$	$$$$$$	$$$$$$	$$$$$$
BUYER	$$$$$$	$$$$$$	$$$$$$	$$$$$$	$$$$$$
BUYER	$$$$$$	$$$$$$	$$$$$$	$$$$$$	$$$$$$
BUYER	$$$$$$	$$$$$$	$$$$$$	$$$$$$	$$$$$$

That way, within seconds, you will know the **Transaction Amount** (Overall) paid by each BUYER to buy each TYPE of Real Estate.

It works the same if you want to know the **CASHFLOW**. In order to do that you just need to use CASHFLOW in the Value Section.

That said, let's solve one simple exercise for this Chapter!

Open file PivotNinjaChapter3ex1.xlsx

Your task in this exercise is to open a Pivot Table Creator. You ARE NOT going to create a Pivot Table yet, just open the Pivot Table Creator.

STEP 1: Select the complete Database (From B3 to I550).

Option 1: You can just click on B3 and drag the mouse until you get to I550

Option 2: Position yourself in B3, hold Ctrl + Shift (Command + Shift if you are on a MacBook) and press Right Arrow once and Down Arrow once.

That way you will have selected the complete Database.

STEP 2: While having the Database selected, click on INSERT tab and the PivotTable

STEP 3: Select whether you want to create your Pivot Table on a New worksheet or an Existing worksheet. I always want my Pivot Tables on a New Worksheet. The hit OK.

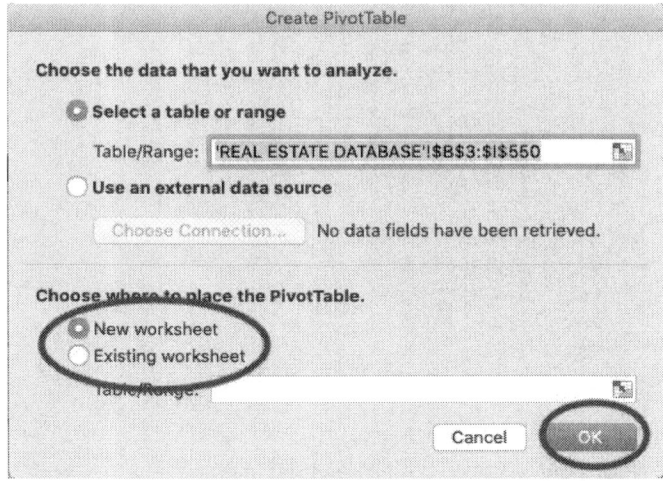

STEP 4: There you have it, your Pivot Table Creator.

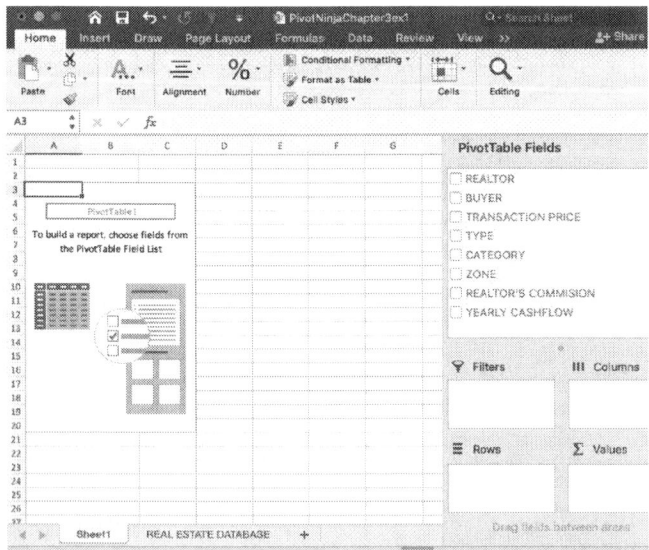

Notice the following things:

- It is on a NEW worksheet (called Sheet1), and it is linked to the Database in the other Worksheet (called REAL ESTATE DATABASE)
- The Pivot Table Creator is there, to the right of your Excel.
- PivotTable Fields are there, just as we discussed it during this chapter, on Top of the Pivot Table Creator.
- There is no Pivot Table yet, you just get the strange section to the left named **PivotTable1**

IMPORTANT NOTE:

If by any means your Pivot Table Creator disappears just follow this:

1) Click inside PivotTable1

2) Go to your Ribbon and click the Pivot Table Analyze tab and then Field List

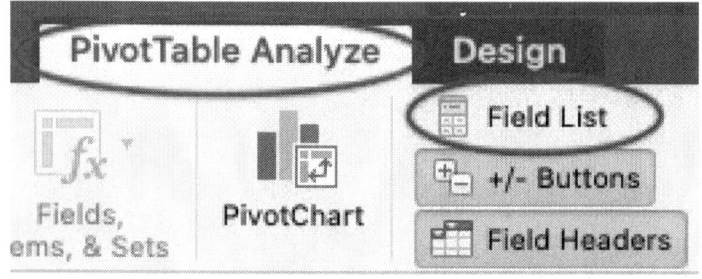

3) There you have your Pivot Table Creator again

CONGRATULATIONS! This is your first step in your journey to become a Pivot Table and Pivot Charts Ninja!

QUICK CHAPTER SUMMARY:

- The Pivot Table Creator is the main tool to develop a Pivot Table
- Pivot Table Fields are the main labels of your Databases
- There are 5 sections: Pivot Table Fields, Filters, Rows, Columns and Values

- You need to put the right Pivot Table Field into the right Section in order to create the Pivot Table you want

CHAPTER 4

PIVOT TABLES WITH 2 VARIABLES

Do you remember when I asked you to get the answer to some questions back in Chapter 2? Those questions are time-consuming if you are not using Pivot Tables but, NOW you are going to answer all of them with my help and, of course, with the help of the Pivot Tables you are going to create!

In this chapter we will focus on Pivot Tables with 2 VARIABLES. So, what is a variable anyway? A variable could be anything: Revenue, buyers, sales executives, transaction price, commission, year, category, etc.

So, when you are trying to answer a question with 2 variables, you will find something like the following questions (taken from Chapter 2, and the exact questions we are going to answer through this chapter):

- Find the total amount of sales (transaction price) made by Ron Weasley
- Find the total amount of money paid (transaction price) by Dragon Real Estate Company

Notice how the first question has Transaction amount and Realtor as the 2 variables. The second question has also Transaction amount but the second variable is the Buyer.

That is what I'm talking about when I say "variables". So, ready or not, here we go!

Open file PivotNinjaChapter4ex1.xlsx

Your job in this exercise is to create a Pivot Table to answer the first question:

Find the total amount of sales (transaction price) made by Ron Weasley

STEP 1: Follow the steps in the previous chapter to display the Pivot Table Creator!

STEP 2: As John Lennon would say "Imagine all the people!". So, imagine all the people and categories in your desired Pivot Table. You have to see it in your mind before you can create it in your computer!

As far as I'm concerned, your Pivot Table should look something like this for you to get an answer to your question.

	SUM OF TRANSACTION PRICE
REALTOR	$$$$
REALTOR	$$$$
REALTOR	$$$$
RON WEASLEY	$$$$
REALTOR	$$$$

REALTOR	$$$$
REALTOR	$$$$

Look how the Realtors are listed on each row, and the ONLY ONE column is the TRASACTION PRICE (Which would be displayed as the sum of all the transaction prices).

STEP 3: Analyze which Field goes into which Section.

You have 2 variables (which are on the Fields): Realtors and Transaction Price

PivotTable Fields

- ☐ REALTOR
- ☐ BUYER
- ☐ TRANSACTION PRICE
- ☐ TYPE

Remember that in STEP 2 **Realto**r were displayed on a list, that means that you want them on **ROWS**.

And because Total Sales (Transaction Price) is the **RESULT (VALUE)** that you want to find, then **Transaction Price** goes into **VALUES** Section:

IMPORTANT NOTE: YOU CAN SKIP COLUMNS AND FILTERS, BUT WITHOUT SOME FIELD ON VALUES SECTION, NOTHING HAPPENS!

In simple words: To create a Pivot Table you will always need to add something to VALUES Section, otherwise you get nothing.

STEP 4: Click, Hold and Drag the correct Fields to the correct Sections!

I want you to:

1) Click, Hold and Drag REALTOR to the ROWS Section and
2) Click, Hold and Drag TRANSACTION PRICE to the VALUES Section

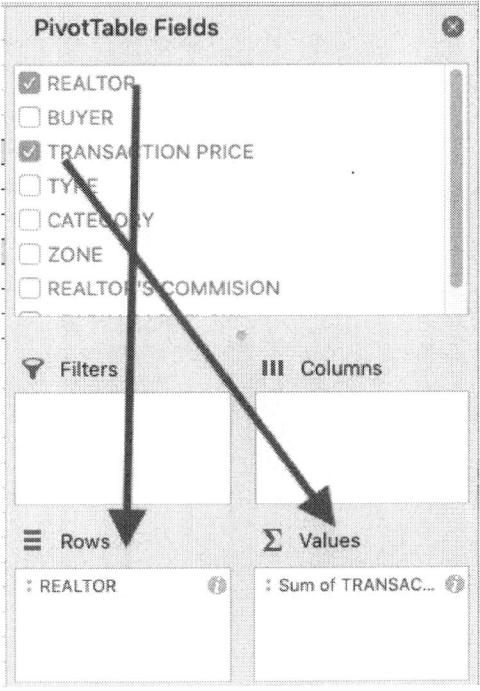

There you have it! You Pivot Table was created Instantly! You have one Realtor by row, and the SUM of THE TRANSACTION PRICES they made (in other words, the total amount of sales)

Row Labels	Sum of TRANSACTION PRICE
Ant-Man	831484
Batman	3058380
Batwoman	18986609
Bumblebee	15052655
Captain America	5291764
Captain Marvel	4844998

(Obviously, you have a much bigger table)

What you need to do is to use the small Filter Icon to find Ron Weasley or to scroll down and find it there

46	Robin Hood	31278976
47	Rocky Balboa	9071205
48	**Ron Weasley**	**10339252**
49	Sarah Connor	2411144
50	Sasuke Uchiha	7504843

So, the answer is:

Ron Weasley sold more than 10 million dollars in properties!

Let's solve the next exercise and the next question!

Open file PivotNinjaChapter4ex2.xlsx

Your job in this exercise is to create a Pivot Table to answer the second question:

Find the total amount of money paid (transaction price) by Dragon Real Estate Company

STEP 1: Follow the steps in the previous chapter to display the Pivot Table Creator!

STEP 2: Imagine your Pivot Table.

Your Pivot Table should look something like this for you to get an answer to your question.

	SUM OF TRANSACTION PRICE
BUYER	$$$$
BUYER	$$$$

BUYER	$$$$
DRAGON REAL ESTATE	$$$$
BUYER	$$$$

STEP 3: Analyze which Field goes into which Section.

You have 2 variables (which are on the Fields): BUYERS and TRANSACTION PRICE

Remember that in STEP 2 **BUYERS** were displayed on a list, that means that you want them on **ROWS.**

And because Total Sales (Transaction Price) is the **RESULT (VALUE)** that you want to find, then **Transaction Price** goes into **VALUES** Section:

STEP 4: Click, Hold and Drag the correct Fields to the correct Sections!

I want you to:

3) Click, Hold and Drag BUYER to the ROWS Section and
4) Click, Hold and Drag TRANSACTION PRICE to the VALUES Section

Row Labels	Sum of TRANSACTION PRICE
Dragon Real Estate Company	95876604
Hogwarts Investing Holding	93583369
Justice League REIT	103949714
Lord of The Real Estate Inc	82799420
Marvell Real Estate Holding	82452473
Star Realtors Inc	65123932
Grand Total	523785512

There you have it! The Transaction amount made by every BUYER, and the answer is:

Dragon Real Estate Company paid almost 96 million dollars to buy properties!

CONGRATULATIONS! You already know how to create Pivot Tables with 2 variables!

Now, try to solve more exercises before continuing with the next Chapter!

MORE EXERCISES:

- PivotNinjaChapter4ex3.xlsx
- PivotNinjaChapter4ex4.xlsx
- PivotNinjaChapter4ex5.xlsx

QUICK CHAPTER SUMMARY:

- The minimum number of Variables to create a Pivot Table is 2
- Remember, you need to visualize your desired layout for the Pivot Table BEFORE you create the Pivot Table itself
- You need to have a clear understanding of the answer you are looking for.

Are you enjoying this book?

Do you think it's easy to understand?

Have the exercises helped you learn faster?

Without knowing your opinion, I won't know if the book has helped you to become a better Excel user.

You can share your thoughts with me by writing a Review

CHAPTER 5

PIVOT TABLES WITH 3 VARIABLES

Now is the right time to increment the difficulty and go to the next level: 3 Variable Pivot Tables

The answers we are going to find are the following:

- How much incoming Cashflow are Justice League REIT and Star Realtors Inc getting from Downtown properties?
- Which Realtor is the best at selling Offices?

NOTICE THE FOLLOWING:

- In the first one, you have Cashflow, Buyer and Zone (3 variables)
- In the second one, you have Realtor, Sales and Type (3 variables)

With that said, it let's go and create some Pivot Tables!

Open file PivotNinjaChapter5ex1.xlsx

Your job in this exercise is to create a Pivot Table to answer the first question:

Find the Cashflow that Justice League REIT and Star Realtors INC are getting from their Downtown Properties

STEP 1: Display the Pivot Table Creator

STEP 2: Imagine your Pivot Table.

Your Pivot Table should look something like this for you to get an answer to your question.

		SOUTH	WEST	**DOWNTOWN**	NORTH	EAST

BUYER	$$$	$$$	$$$	$$$	$$$
JUSTICE LEAGUE REIT	$$$	$$$	**$$$**	$$$	$$$
BUYER	$$$	$$$	$$$	$$$	$$$
STAR REALTORS INC	$$$	$$$	**$$$**	$$$	$$$
BUYER	$$$	$$$	$$$	$$$	$$$

IMPORTANT:

Notice how your Pivot Table MUST display the Buyers AND the ZONES at the same time! While showing the corresponding Cashflow for each part of the grid.

STEP 3: Analyze which Field goes into which Section.

You have 3 variables (which are on the Fields): **BUYERS, ZONES and CASHFLOW**

- Remember that in STEP 2 **BUYERS** were displayed on a list, that means that you want them on **ROWS**.

- Also, the ZONES are at the Top of each COLUMN, so you want to put **ZONES** into the **COLUMN** Section
- And because CASHFLOW is the **RESULT (VALUE)** that you want to find, then **CASHFLOW** goes into **VALUES** Section:

STEP 4: Click, Hold and Drag the correct Fields to the correct Sections!

BUYER in ROWS

ZONES in COLUMNS

CASHFLOW in VALUES

Sum of YEARLY CASHFLOW	Column Labels		
Row Labels	DOWNTON	EAST	NORT
Dragon Real Estate Company	1888875.06	1206155.18	169!
Hogwarts Investing Holding	1648225.65	1463645.87	129!
Justice League REIT	1928739.83	1505699.75	218(
Lord of The Real Estate Inc	1974404.43	891323.61	149:
Marvell Real Estate Holding	1501428.25	1199354.59	182(
Star Realtors Inc	1027889.35	1094139.15	111.
Grand Total	9969562.57	7360318.15	961!

There you have it!

Justice League REIT bought 1.9 Million dollars in Downtown and Star Realtor INC bought 1 Million dollars in Downtown

Let's solve the next exercise!

Open file PivotNinjaChapter5ex2.xlsx

Your job in this exercise is to create a Pivot Table to answer the next question:

Which Realtor is the best at selling Offices?

STEP 1: Display the Pivot Table Creator

STEP 2: Imagine your Pivot Table.

Your Pivot Table should look something like this for you to get an answer to your question.

	HOUSES	DUPLEX	STORES	**OFFICES**
TOP REALTOR	$$$	$$$	$$$	**$$$**

REALTOR	$$$	$$$	$$$	$$$
REALTOR	$$$	$$$	$$$	$$$
REALTOR	$$$	$$$	$$$	$$$
REALTOR	$$$	$$$	$$$	$$$

STEP 3: Analyze which Field goes into which Section.

You have 3 variables (which are on the Fields): **REALTOR, TYPE and TRANSACTION PRICE**

STEP 4: Click, Hold and Drag the correct Fields to the correct Sections!

REALTOR in ROWS

TYPE in COLUMNS

TRANSACTION PRICE in VALUES

And now you have a GIANT Pivot Table like this one (Obviously I'm just inserting the Screenshot of one little part)

Sum of TRANSACTI	Column						
Row Labels	APARTMEN	CONDO	DUPLEX	HOUSE	OFFICE	STORE	Grand Total
Ant-Man		831484					831484
Batman	793128	818345			1446907		3058380
Batwoman	2103230	5178824	3375087	830827	2976596	4522045	18986609
Bumblebee	776810	2801996	5071347	1163779	3575502	1663221	15052655
Captain America	616560			2225599	1764162	685443	5291764
Captain Marvel	671459		1382702	1348398	1442439		4844998
Daredevil	5488743		1173148	2797861	5643273	1117972	16220997
Doc Savage	2632963	2169991	4717185	1946151	1067104	951000	13484394

But you have one BIG problem: The Pivot Table sorted the values by the Realtor's Name! And you need to sort that table by the largest sales in Office properties.

SOLUTION:

STEP 1: Position yourself anywhere in the OFFICE COLUMN

HOUSE	OFFICE	STORE	Grand Tot:
			831484
	1446907		3058380
830827	2976596	4522045	18986609
1163779	3575502	1663221	15052655
	1764162	685443	5291764
1348398	1442439		4844998

STEP 2: Right click in the same cell (in the Office Column) and click **SORT** and the

SORT LARGEST TO SMALLEST

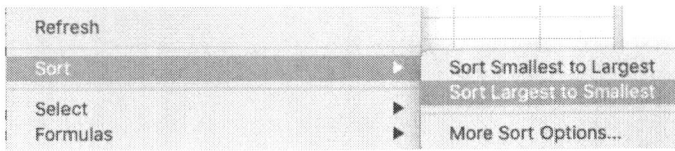

There you have it!

Sum of TRANSACTI Colum						
Row Labels	APARTMI	CONDO	DUPLEX	HOUSE	OFFICE	STO
Daredevil	5488743		1173148	2797861	5643273	1
Iron Man	2216306	456309	2163731	6237825	5084181	4
Robin Hood	5025855	7421627	834412	8348697	4654353	4
Bumblebee	776810	2801996	5071347	1163779	3575502	1

Daredevil was the best at selling Offices, selling 5.6 million dollars!

CONGRATULATIONS! You are really moving forward in your journey. Soon, you are going to become a Pivot Tables and Pivot Charts Ninja!

MORE EXERCISES:

- PivotNinjaChapter5ex3.xlsx

- PivotNinjaChapter5ex4.xlsx

QUICK CHAPTER SUMMARY:

- 3 Variable Pivot Tables are the most used. So, if you master them, you can solve virtually 80% of the questions regarding a database.
- The "Sort" option is a super handy tool. Remember that it sorts the COLUMN, not the row.
- You can sort easily from Largest to Smallest and from Smallest to Largest.

CHAPTER 6

ADDITIONAL TOOL: "SUMMARIZE BY"

For this Chapter we are going to use the same exercises as the previous one because you are going to learn how to implement the "Summarize By" tool.

Previously, each time we talked about VALUES Section, we were displaying the **SUM of the Transactions**: Sum of Transaction Price, Sum of Cashflow, Sum of commissions earned, etc.

With "Summarize By" tool you are able to not display the Sum, but to choose between the **AVERAGE, COUNT, MAXIMUM, MINIMUM** and other options.

In plain English, instead of just answering:

- Find the Cashflow that Justice League REIT and Star Realtors INC are getting from their Downtown Properties

With a few clicks you could also answer:

- Find the **AVERAGE** Property Cashflow that Justice League REIT and Star Realtors INC are getting from their Downtown Properties
- Find the **NUMBER OF PROPERTIES** that Justice League REIT and Star Realtors INC have in Downtown
- Find the **MAXIMUM** Cashflow a property gives to Justice League REIT and Star Realtors INC in Downtown
- Find the **MINIMUM** Cashflow a property gives to Justice League REIT and Star Realtors INC in Downtown

Open file PivotNinjaChapter6ex1.xlsx

Your job in this exercise is to create a Pivot Table to answer the next question:

Find the <u>AVERAGE</u> Property Cashflow that Justice League REIT and Star Realtors INC are getting from their Downtown Properties

STEP 1: You already have your Pivot Table, so, go to the VALUES SECTION of the Pivot Table Creator and click the "I" icon

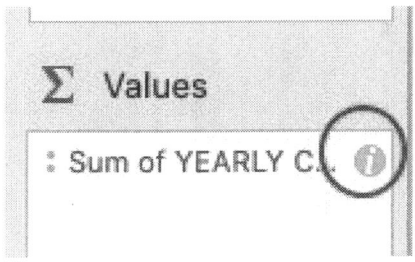

STEP 2: You are going to be presented with a display like this one:

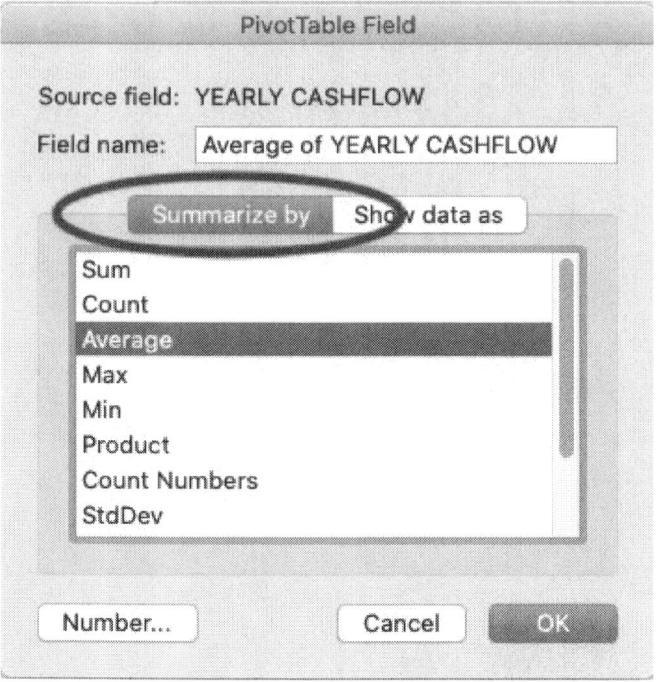

Just select **"Summarize by"**, then click on **"AVERAGE"** and then hit **OK**.

STEP 3: There you have it, now your Pivot Table is displaying the **AVERAGE Cashflow** for each of the variables.

Average of YEARLY CASHFLOW	Column Labels	
Row Labels	DOWNTON	EAST
Dragon Real Estate Company	69958.34	70950.30
Hogwarts Investing Holding	74919.35	77033.99
Justice League REIT	68883.57	62737.49
Lord of The Real Estate Inc	70514.44	68563.35
Marvell Real Estate Holding	88319.31	74959.66
Star Realtors Inc	68525.96	72942.61
Grand Total	72770.53	70772.29

Justice League REIT averages $68,883 of Cashflow per Property in Downtown

and Star Realtor INC averages $68,525 of Cashflow per Property in Downtown

And what about knowing how many properties they have? Let's figure it out!

Open file PivotNinjaChapter6ex2.xlsx

Your job in this exercise is to create a Pivot Table to answer the next question:

Find the <u>NUMBER OF PROPERTIES</u> that Justice League REIT and Star Realtors INC have in Downtown

STEP 1: You already have your Pivot Table, so, go to the VALUES SECTION of the

Pivot Table Creator and click the "I" icon

STEP 2: You are going to be presented with the same display as the previous exercise. This time just select **"Summarize by"**, then click on **"COUNT"** and then hit **OK**.

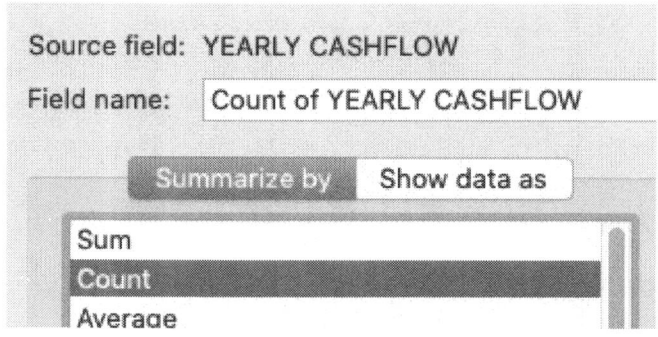

STEP 3: There you have it, now your Pivot Table is displaying the **COUNT (NUMBER) OF PROPERTIES** for each of the variables.

Count of YEARLY CASHFLOW	Column Labels		
Row Labels	DOWNTON	EAST	NOR
Dragon Real Estate Company	27	17	
Hogwarts Investing Holding	22	19	
Justice League REIT	28	24	
Lord of The Real Estate Inc	28	13	
Marvell Real Estate Holding	17	16	
Star Realtors Inc	15	15	
Grand Total	137	104	

Justice League REIT owns 28 properties in Downtown

and Star Realtor INC owns 15 properties in Downtown

The same principle applies to MAXIMUM and MINIMUM, so go ahead and solve the exercises!

MORE EXERCISES:

- PivotNinjaChapter6ex3.xlsx
- PivotNinjaChapter6ex4.xlsx

QUICK CHAPTER SUMMARY:

- With just a few clicks more, after creating a Pivot Table, you can answer a whole lot more of questions
- Questions regarding AERAGES, MAXIMUM, MINIMUM and COUNTS are at your fingertips with the "Summarize By" Tool

CHAPTER 7
ADDITIONAL TOOL:
"SHOW DATA AS"

Just as the previous chapter, you are going to learn one additional tool that is called "Show Data As". With this tool we are done with the Pivot Table part of the book, so in the next chapter you will learn about Slicers and then about Pivot Charts.

With "Show Data As" the main focus is to express the Values in percentages, but it is not as simple as it sounds. Remember that Pivot Tables are flexible, thus the percentages will be flexible also.

We will focus in the **3 main Percentage** options:

- **Percentage of the Grand Total**
- **Percentage of the Column**

- **Percentage of the Row**

To make this concept more understandable, let me use the same exercise as the previous chapter. By using the same exercise you get the benefit of already knowing the previous steps and being familiar to that Pivot Table, and because of that you can focus on the new part of the exercise, the "Show Data As" tool.

If you don't mind, let's start!

Open file PivotNinjaChapter7ex1.xlsx

Your job in this exercise is to create a Pivot Table to answer the next question:

Find the Property Cashflow that Justice League REIT and Star Realtors INC are getting from their Downtown Properties <u>AND SHOW IT AS A PERCENTAGE OF THE TOTAL CASHFLOW</u>

STEP 1: You already have your Pivot Table, so, go to the VALUES SECTION of the Pivot Table Creator and click the "I" icon

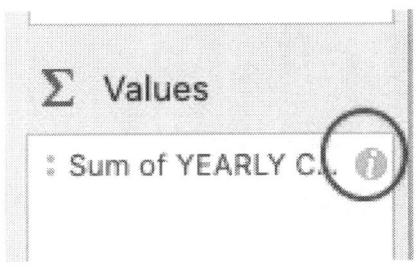

STEP 2: You are going to be presented with a display like this one:

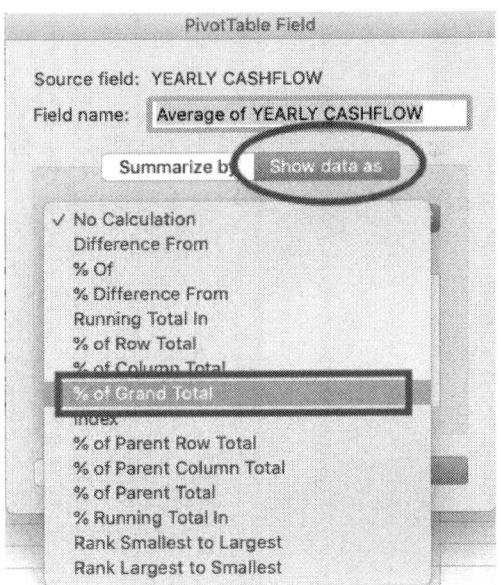

Select "**SHOW DATA AS**", then display the list that says "No Calculation", the click on "**% OF THE GRAND TOTAL**" and then hit **OK**.

WHAT DOES THAT MEAN?

It means that your values are **NOT** going to be shown in dollars. Instead, they are going to be displayed as a percentage. Moreover, the Pivot Table is going to consider the Total Cashflow of the **ENTIRE DATABASE** as 100%, and then it is going to show the values accordingly.

STEP 3: There you have it, now your Pivot Table is displaying the **PERCENTAGE OF THE GRAND TOTAL** for each of the variables.

Sum of YEARLY CASHFLOW	Column Labels					
Row Labels	DOWNTON	EAST	NORTH	SOUTH	WEST	Grand Total
Dragon Real Estate Company	4.76%	3.04%	4.28%	2.33%	3.66%	18.07%
Hogwarts Investing Holding	4.16%	3.69%	3.28%	2.47%	3.95%	17.55%
Justice League REIT	4.87%	3.80%	5.52%	2.54%	3.44%	20.16%
Lord of The Real Estate Inc	4.98%	2.25%	3.76%	1.24%	3.17%	15.39%
Marvell Real Estate Holding	3.79%	3.03%	4.61%	1.80%	3.31%	16.54%
Star Realtors Inc	2.59%	2.76%	2.81%	1.84%	2.29%	12.29%
Grand Total	25.15%	18.57%	24.25%	12.21%	19.82%	100.00%

NOTICE the following facts:

- Because we are talking about the % of the Grand Total, the figures INSIDE the square are going to be equal to 100%. (As an example, **Justice League REIT is getting 4.87% of the Overall Cashflow from their Downtown properties**)
- Because we are talking about the % of the Grand Total, if you add the figures IN THE LAST ROW they are going to be equal to 100% (**Downtown properties provide 25.15% of the Cashflow, buy South properties provide only 12.21%**)
- Because we are talking about the % of the Grand Total, the figures IN THE LAST COLUMNS are going to be equal to 100% also (**Justice League get 20.16% of the Overall Cashflow, but Star Realtors get only 12.29%**)

That is how you read Pivot Table that is shown as a Percentage of the Grand Total.

Now let's move to the "Percentage of the Column"

Open file PivotNinjaChapter7ex2.xlsx

Your job in this exercise is to create a Pivot Table to answer the next question:

Find the Property Cashflow that Justice League REIT and Star Realtors INC are getting from their Downtown Properties <u>AND SHOW IT AS A PERCENTAGE OF EACH ZONE!</u>

STEP 1: Same Step 1 as the previous Exercise

STEP 2: You are going to be presented with the same display.

Select "**SHOW DATA AS**," then display the list that says "No Calculation", the click on "**% OF THE COLUMN TOTAL**" and then hit **OK**.

```
Running Total In
% of Row Total
✓ % of Column Total
% of Grand Total
Index
```

WHY DID WE CHOOSE "% OF THE COLUMN TOTAL"?

Because, if you look at the Pivot Table you already have, you will notice that the ZONES are displayed as COLUMNS.

Sum of YEARLY CASHFLOW	Column Labels			
Row Labels	DOWNTON	EAST	NORTH	SOUTH
Dragon Real Estate Company	1888875	1206155	1695064	9241
Hogwarts Investing Holding	1648226	1463646	1299205	9786
Justice League REIT	1928740	1505700	2186853	10063
Lord of The Real Estate Inc	1974404	891324	1491681	4899
Marvell Real Estate Holding	1501428	1199355	1828644	7131
Star Realtors Inc	1027889	1094139	1114355	7276

Therefore, as we want the **PERCENTAGE OF EACH ZONE**, we need to choose the **"% OF THE COLUMNS TOTAL"**

WHAT DOES THAT MEAN?

It means that your values are NOT going to be shown in dollars. Instead, they are going to be displayed as a percentage OF EACH ZONE (COLUMN), so the Pivot Table is going to consider EACH ZONE as 100%.

STEP 3: There you have your Pivot Table

Sum of YEARLY CASHFLOW	Column Labels					
Row Labels	DOWNTON	EAST	NORTH	SOUTH	WEST	Grand Total
Dragon Real Estate Company	18.95%	16.39%	17.63%	19.09%	18.45%	18.07%
Hogwarts Investing Holding	16.53%	19.89%	13.51%	20.22%	19.94%	17.55%
Justice League REIT	19.35%	20.46%	22.74%	20.79%	17.35%	20.16%
Lord of The Real Estate Inc	19.80%	12.11%	15.51%	10.12%	15.97%	15.39%
Marvell Real Estate Holding	15.06%	16.29%	19.02%	14.73%	16.72%	16.54%
Star Realtors Inc	10.31%	14.87%	11.59%	15.03%	11.57%	12.29%
Grand Total	100.00%	100.00%	100.00%	100.00%	100.00%	100.00%

NOTICE the following facts:

- Because we are talking about the % of the Column Total, each zone adds up to 100%. (As an example, **Downtown Properties** give X amount of dollars in Cashflow. **Justice League REIT is getting 19.35% of that Cashflow and Star Realtors is getting just 10.31% of the Cashflow given by all the Downton Properties)**

- Because we are talking about the % of the Column Total, all the figures IN THE LAST ROW are going to display 100% **(If you sum all the Downtown percentages you will get 100%, if you do the same with all the zones, you will get 100% on each column)**

- Because we are talking about the % of the Column Total, the figures IN THE LAST COLUMN represent the OVERALL CASHFLOW. Notice how this last COLUMN IS EXACTLY THE SAME AS THE LAST COLUMN IN THE PREVIOUS EXERCISE, because in this column we are talking about the OVERALL CASHFLOW also **(Justice League get 20.16% of the Overall Cashflow, but Star Realtors get only 12.29%)**

That is how you read Pivot Table that is shown as a Percentage of the Column Total.

Now let's move to the "Percentage of the Row"

Open file PivotNinjaChapter7ex3.xlsx

Your job in this exercise is to create a Pivot Table to answer the next question:

Find the Property Cashflow that Justice League REIT and Star Realtors INC are getting from their Downtown Properties <u>AND SHOW IT AS A PERCENTAGE OF EACH COMPANY!</u>

STEP 1: Same Step 1 as the previous Exercise

STEP 2: You are going to be presented with the same display.

Select "**SHOW DATA AS**", then display the list that says "No Calculation", the click on "**% OF THE ROW TOTAL**" and then hit **OK**.

> % Difference From
> Running Total In
> ✓ % of Row Total
> % of Column Total
> % of Grand Total

WHY DID WE CHOOSE "% OF THE COLUMN TOTAL"?

Because, if you look at the Pivot Table you already have, you will notice that the COMPANIES are displayed as ROWS.

Sum of YEARLY CASHFLOW	Column Labels			
Row Labels	DOWNTON	EAST	NORTH	SOUTH
Dragon Real Estate Company	1888875	1206155	1695064	9241:
Hogwarts Investing Holding	1648226	1463646	1299205	9786.
Justice League REIT	1928740	1505700	2186853	10063.
Lord of The Real Estate Inc	1974404	891324	1491681	4899:
Marvell Real Estate Holding	1501428	1199355	1828644	7131:
Star Realtors Inc	1027889	1094139	1114355	7276.
Grand Total	9969563	7360318	9615802	48399

Therefore, as we want the **PERCENTAGE**

OF EACH COMPANY, we need to choose the "**% OF THE ROW TOTAL**"

WHAT DOES THAT MEAN?

It means that your values are **NOT** going to be shown in dollars. Instead, they are going to be displayed as a percentage **OF EACH COMPAMY (ROW)**, so the Pivot Table is going to consider **EACH COMPANY** as 100%.

STEP 3: There you have your Pivot Table

Sum of YEARLY CASHFLOW	Column Labels					
Row Labels	DOWNTON	EAST	NORTH	SOUTH	WEST	Grand Total
Dragon Real Estate Company	26.37%	16.84%	23.66%	12.90%	20.24%	100.00%
Hogwarts Investing Holding	23.69%	21.04%	18.67%	14.07%	22.53%	100.00%
Justice League REIT	24.13%	18.84%	27.36%	12.59%	17.07%	100.00%
Lord of The Real Estate Inc	32.35%	14.61%	24.44%	8.03%	20.57%	100.00%
Marvell Real Estate Holding	22.90%	18.29%	27.89%	10.88%	20.04%	100.00%
Star Realtors Inc	21.09%	22.45%	22.87%	14.93%	18.65%	100.00%
Grand Total	25.15%	18.57%	24.25%	12.21%	19.82%	100.00%

(Notice how all the "100%" are now in the last column, not in the last row. That is because % of the Row Total is kind of the inverse of % of the Column Total)

NOTICE the following facts:

- Because we are talking about the % of the Row Total, each COMPANY adds up to 100%. (As an example, **Dragon Real Estate Company gets X amount of dollars in Cashflow. N NORTH Properties are providing 23.66% of that Cashflow and SOUTH properties are providing just 12.90% of the Cashflow gotten by Dragon Real Estate)**
- Because we are talking about the % of the Row Total, all the figures IN THE LAST COLUMN are going to display 100% **(If you sum all the Hogwarts Investing Holding percentages you will get 100%, if you do the same with all the Companies, you will get 100% on each row)**
- Because we are talking about the % of the Row Total, the figures IN THE LAST ROW represent the OVERALL CASHFLOW **(Downton properties**

give 25.15% of the Overall Cashflow, but South properties give only 12.21% of the Overall Cashflow)

That is how you read Pivot Table that is shown as a Percentage of the Row Total.

IMPORTANT NOTE:

I'M SORRY IF I USED THE SAME EXERCISE OVER AND OVER, BUT YOU MAY AGREE WITH ME THAT IN ORDER TO BETTER EXPLAIN ALL THE DETAILS OF "SHOW DATA AS" AND "SUMMARIZE BY" IT WAS FAR BETTER TO FOCUS ON THE SAME PIVOT TABLE AND RE-SHAPE IT WITH DIFFERENT VALUES.

I'M SURE YOU GOT MORE OUT OF IT THAT WAY!

So, now it is time for you to solve the following exercises.

MORE EXERCISES:

- PivotNinjaChapter7ex4.xlsx
- PivotNinjaChapter7ex5.xlsx
- PivotNinjaChapter7ex5.xlsx

QUICK CHAPTER SUMMARY:

- The "Show Data As" Tool is one of the best tools to get even better insight than a simple Pivot Table would give.
- The main 3 outputs you can get with this tool are: Percentage of the Grand Total, Column Total and Row Total
- Remember to be aware in every moment about which one you are using, because the result you get and the reasoning behind that result would be different with each one of them.

CHAPTER 8
SLICERS (ADVANCED FILTERS)

You are almost there! In no time you will complete your journey as a Pivot Table and Pivot Chart Ninja.

In this chapter you will use Slicers. So, I call Slicers "Advanced Filter" because their purpose is to sort and MANIPULATE the Pivot Table and display JUST the information you selected in the Slicers.

That said, I want you to really understand the idea with the following 2 statements.

Pivot Tables are created though the information of a Database, so any Pivot Table is a summary itself.

Slicers allow to further summarize and filter that same Pivot Table, and at the same time, allow to change those filters fast, just in case you need even deeper information

In plain English, Pivot Tables become even more powerful when you use Slicers!

WHERE DOES SLICERS COME FROM?

You can create Slicers out of any of the Pivot Table Fields that you have. Just to follow the Database of this book, that means that you can create:

- Slicer for Buyers
- Slicer for Zones
- Slicer for Realtors
- Slicer for Categories
- Slicer for Types

NOTE: Slicer for dollar amounts (As transaction prices and Cashflow) are not recommended, because usually those fields go into the Values Section.

HOW DOES A SLICER LOOK LIKE?

Well, a Slicer looks exactly like this!

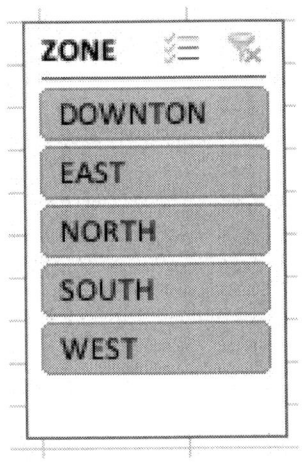

This one is a Zone Slicer. And what does that mean? It means that you can manipulate the Pivot Table to show the results of the zones that you want to see and remove the ones that you don't want to see! This is so great.

HOW DOES A PIVOT TABLES CHANGE VISUALLY WHEN USING A SLICER?

It changes in 2 different ways:

- If the Slicer you are using (as an example, Zones) IS in the Columns or Rows of the Pivot Table, then your Pivot Table will hide the Zones that you don't select in the slicer and leave at sight the ones you choose. So, the Pivot Table layout will change in this example.
- If the Slicer you are using IS NOT in the Columns or Rows of the Pivot Table, what you are going to see changed are the Values in the Pivot Tables (the numbers, dollars, averages, etc.) because the Pivot Table will consider only the Zones selected in your Slicer.
- Thirdly, you can have a mix of both changes.

HOW DO I CONTROL THE SLICER? (IMPORTANT)

You have 3 ways to control your Slicers: Regular Click, Click while holding Control (Command on Mac) and Click while holding Shift.

REGULAR CLICK:

Following the previous example with the Zones Slicer, if you just click one of the Zones, you will select that one and that is it. If you click another Zone, you will deselect the previous one in order to select the new Zone.

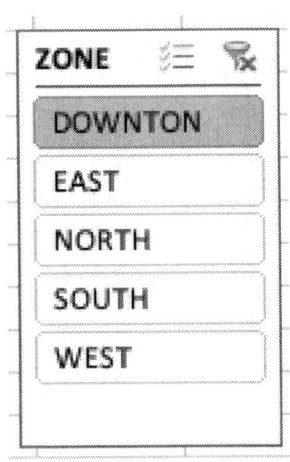

So, with regular click you are allowed to select one Zone at a time.

CLICK WHILE HOLDING CTRL (COMMAND on Mac):

If you do it this way, you are allowed to select MORE than one Zone. So, if you click in Downtown, Hold Ctrl and click in North, you will select both of them

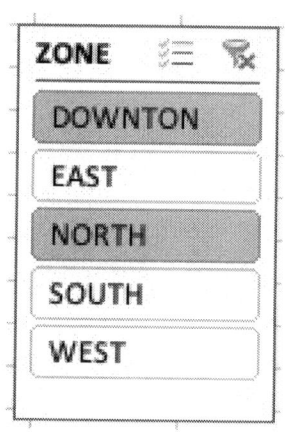

CLICK WHILE HOLDING SHIFT:

If you do it this way, you will select all the zones that are in between of your clicks. So, if you click in Downtown, Hold Shift and click in North, you will select from Downtown to North, including East.

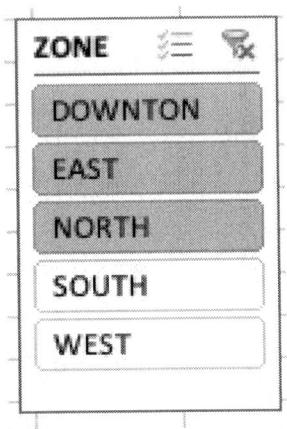

That said, let's start our 2 exercises. You will face one exercise where the Slicers ARE in the Columns and Rows of the Pivot Table and another exercise where the Slicers ARE NOT in the Pivot Table Columns nor Rows.

Open file PivotNinjaChapter8ex1.xlsx

Your job in this exercise is to create the following Pivot Table

Create a Pivot Table that shows the Total amount Paid by each Company on each Type of property

Then, manipulate that Pivot Table with 2 Slicers:

Buyer and Type

STEP 1: Create the Pivot Table! You already know how to do it

STEP 2: You are going to have a Pivot Table like this one (but with more columns and rows). With Buyers in the Rows and Type in the Columns.

Row Labels	APARTMENT	CONDO	DUPLEX
Dragon Real Estate Company	19029218	12053731	18604525
Hogwarts Investing Holding	21914288	11093679	18414619
Justice League REIT	14246656	16719819	20414676
Lord of The Real Estate Inc	14351566	15295110	13725148
Marvell Real Estate Holding	7414831	7675337	15959364

STEP 3: Create the Slicers. To do that follow these instructions:

- Click on the Pivot Table
- On the Ribbon (upper part of Excel) select **Pivot Table Analyze** and the click **Insert Slicer**

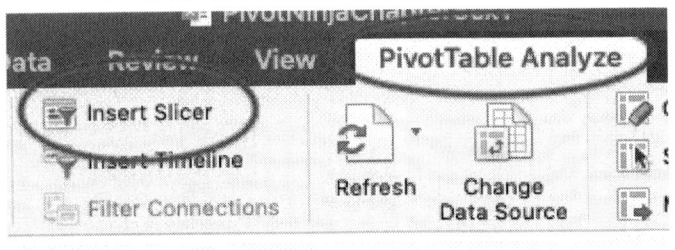

- Select BUYER and TYPE to create both Slicers at the same time

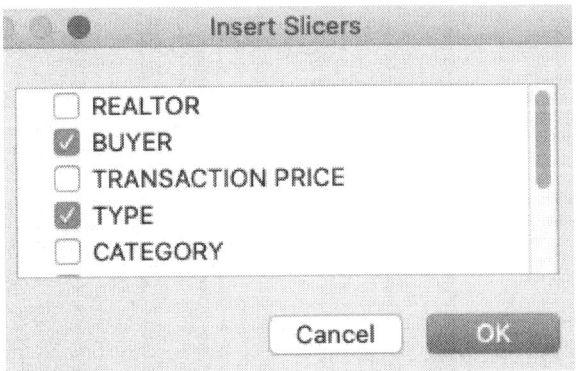

- There you have them! Both Slicers were created instantly

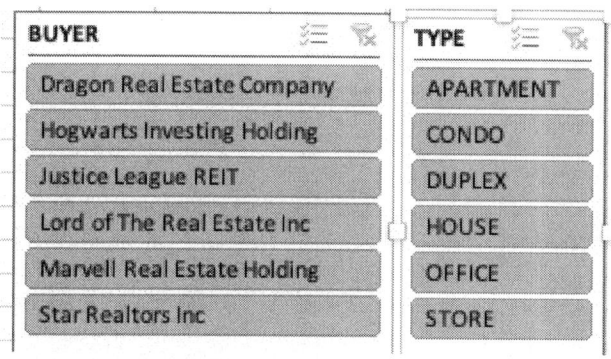

MANIPULATION #1: Just show Hogwarts Investing Holding, Lord of Real Estate and Star Realtors, along with Apartments, Duplex and Offices.

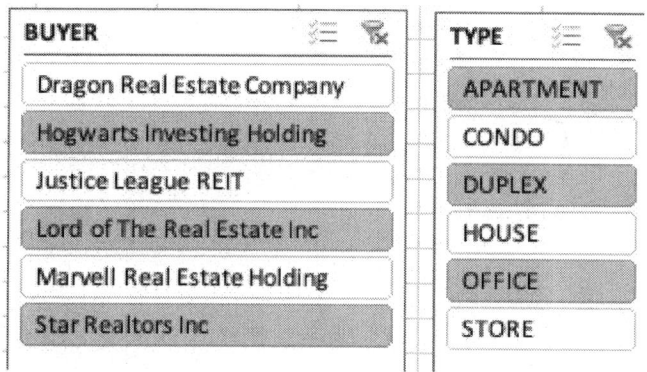

You'll get a Pivot Table like this one!

Sum of TRANSACTION PRICE	Column Labels			
Row Labels	APARTMENT	DUPLEX	OFFICE	Grand Total
Hogwarts Investing Holding	21914288	18414619	14803299	55132206
Lord of The Real Estate Inc	14351566	13725148	10626944	38703658
Star Realtors Inc	7834752	8880229	9381475	26096456
Grand Total	44100606	41019996	34811718	119932320

Notice how everything else disappeared of sight, that way you have a clean Pivot Table displaying just what you want.

MANIPULATION #2: Just show Houses and Stores of Dragon Real Estate Company.

EXCEL PIVOT TABLES AND PIVOT CHARTS NINJA

Sum of TRANSACTION PRICE	Column Labels		
Row Labels	HOUSE	STORE	Grand Total
Dragon Real Estate Company	13726334	13156872	26883206
Grand Total	13726334	13156872	26883206

To delete the filters (if you want to do so) just click on these icons

That's it! Let's continue with the next exercise!

Open file PivotNinjaChapter8ex2.xlsx

Your job in this exercise is to create the following Pivot Table

Create a Pivot Table that shows the Total amount Paid by each Company on each Type of property

Then, manipulate that Pivot Table with 2

Slicers:

Year and Zone

STEP 1: Create the Pivot Table! You already know how to do it

STEP 2: You are going to have a Pivot Table like this one (but with more columns and rows). With Buyers in the Rows and Type in the Columns.

Sum of TRANSACTION PRICE	Column Labels			
Row Labels	APARTMENT	CONDO	DUPLEX	HOUSE
Dragon Real Estate Company	19029218	12053731	18604525	13726334
Hogwarts Investing Holding	21914288	11093679	18414619	14262440
Justice League REIT	14246656	16719819	20414676	16870366
Lord of The Real Estate Inc	14351566	15295110	13725148	10892864
Marvell Real Estate Holding	7414831	7675337	15959364	15824449
Star Realtors Inc	7834752	10356099	8880229	14263138
Grand Total	84791311	73193775	95998561	85839591

STEP 3: Now, follow the Step 3 in the previous exercise to insert two Slicers: **YEAR** and **ZONE**

EXCEL PIVOT TABLES AND PIVOT CHARTS NINJA

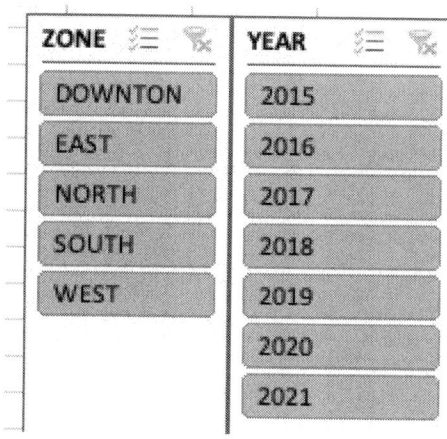

MANIPULATION #1: Show the results for EAST Zone and YEAR 2015

Sum of TRANSACTION PRICE	Column Labels			
Row Labels	APARTMENT	CONDO	DUPLEX	HOUSE
Dragon Real Estate Company	671459			
Hogwarts Investing Holding	759316		2161704	484128
Justice League REIT	838496	651206	1464994	836652
Lord of The Real Estate Inc		829994		
Marvell Real Estate Holding	653702		1276957	
Star Realtors Inc	1440185			
Grand Total	4363158	1481200	4903655	1320780

Look how the Pivot Table layout remained the same, but the Results (Values) inside the Pivot Table were changed, just including the East Zone properties that were bought in 2015

MANIPULATION #2: Show the results for SOUTH and WEST Zones in YEARS 2019 and 2020

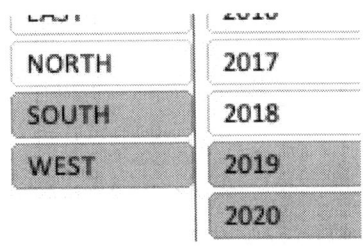

Sum of TRANSACTION PRICE	Column Labels			
Row Labels	APARTMENT	CONDO	DUPLEX	HOUSE
Dragon Real Estate Company	1289697		978352	
Hogwarts Investing Holding	1297654	4000123		2594840
Justice League REIT		715848	2208694	1291397
Lord of The Real Estate Inc	2458082	1227860		1627902
Marvell Real Estate Holding	498513	1368536	1351935	4460354
Star Realtors Inc	720653	1447148	560954	420821
Grand Total	6264599	8759415	5099935	10395314

Same thing, the Pivot Table layout is the same, but the values are including what you want and excluding what you don't want.

CONGRATULATIONS! You have a clear understanding on Slicers. The. Next chapter is going to be all about Pivot Charts.

MORE EXERCISES:

- PivotNinjaChapter8ex3.xlsx
- PivotNinjaChapter8eX4.xlsx

QUICK CHAPTER SUMMARY:

- Slicers are the way to extract more information from a Pivot Table

- Slicers are the fastest way to sort and manipulate a Pivot Table
- Slicers can change the layout of your Pivot Table and/or the Values you get
- Remember to use Ctrl (Command on Mac) and Shift to select or deselect the items of a Slicer

CHAPTER 9

PIVOT CHARTS

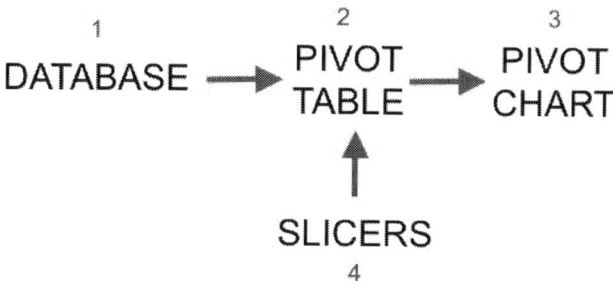

As you remember, I told you that Slicers were the last part of the Pivot Table Creation Process (and they are), but I noticed that is so much easier to explain Pivot Charts once you know how to use Slicers. So, now that you are done with Slicers, let's start with the final part of the book: Pivot Charts!

Pivot Charts are easy if you already know how to handle Pivot Tables and Slicers, nevertheless, you need to be aware that you are not going to learn everything about charts here. If you want to truly become a Charts Ninja, I have a great book called Excel Charts and Graphs Ninja, you can use it to enhance your Charting ability.

That said, you will learn a lot about charts here. Let's start with the exercise.

Open file PivotNinjaChapter9ex1.xlsx

Your job in this exercise is to create the following Pivot Table

Create a Pivot Table that shows the Total amount Paid by each Company each Year

Then, create a Pivot Chart with it

STEP 1: Create the Pivot Table! You already know how to do it

STEP 2: You are going to have a Pivot Table like this one (but with more columns and rows). With Buyers in the Rows and Years in the Columns.

Sum of TRANSACTION PRICE	Column Labels			
Row Labels	2015	2016	2017	2018
Dragon Real Estate Company	7917225	18535966	16862013	14149854
Hogwarts Investing Holding	9074975	6589130	13043342	15074137
Justice League REIT	18524824	15505086	15281981	11493220
Lord of The Real Estate Inc	5156396	11993073	15426213	11357345

STEP 3: Click anywhere inside the Pivot Table, go to **PivotTable Analyze Tab** and click on **Pivot Chart**

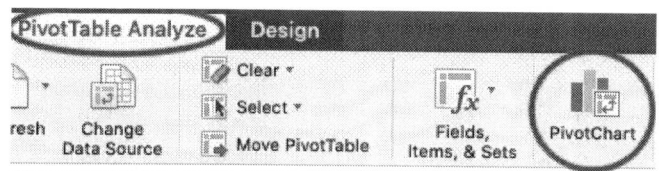

STEP 4: There you have, your Pivot Chart was created. Although it is going to be ugly and cluttered, but it doesn't matter at this moment because latter on this chapter we will declutter it.

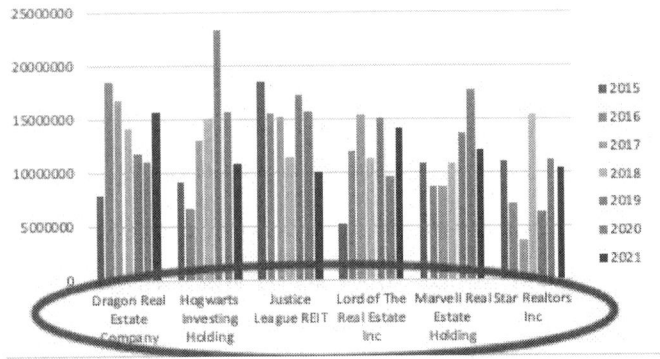

IMPORTANT NOTE: Look how the bars are gathered **BY BUYER**. Each bar represents one **YEAR** but they are in groups by buyer.

So, what happens if we want to show the data in **YEAR** groups? Then do the following.

STEP 5: Click anywhere inside the Chart, Click **DESIGN Tab** and the **Switch Row/Column**

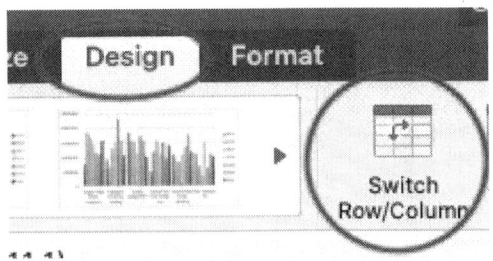

There you have it. Now each bar represents one BUYER and this time, the groups were created by YEAR

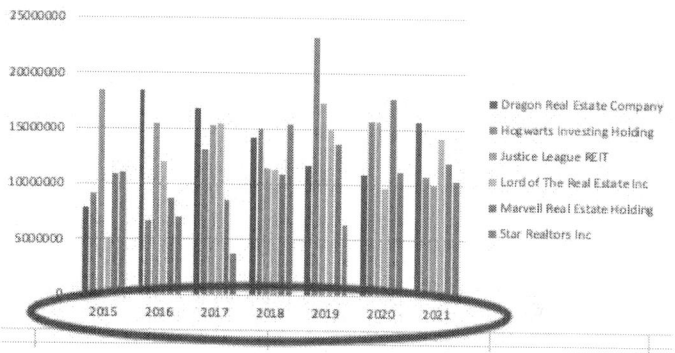

IMPORTANT NOTE:

This is a Bar Chart, and it is a great simple tool. But what if you want to create a line chart? Let's look at it in the next exercise.

Open file PivotNinjaChapter9ex2.xlsx

Your job in this exercise is to create the following Pivot Table

Create a Pivot Table that shows the Total Cashflow created by each Type each Year

Then, create a Pivot Chart with it

STEP 1: Create the Pivot Table! You already know how to do it

STEP 2: You are going to have a Pivot Table like this one

Sum of YEARLY CASHFLOW	Column Labels			
Row Labels	2015	2016	2017	2018
APARTMENT	980229	870173	1018569	616264
CONDO	398128	737799	652579	935346
DUPLEX	1209966	1398331	1028740	979990
HOUSE	947375	909141	1042413	1063774

STEP 3: Click anywhere inside the Pivot Table, go to **PivotTable Analyze Tab** and click on **Pivot Chart**

STEP 4: There you have, your Pivot Chart was created.

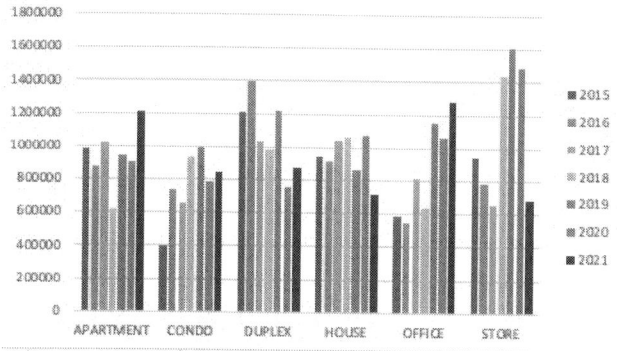

STEP 5: Click anywhere inside the Chart, Click **DESIGN Tab** and the **Switch Row/Column.** Now you have them in groups of years

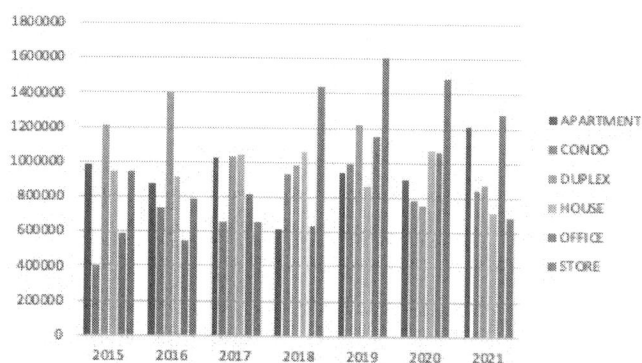

STEP 6: TO CHANGE TO A LINE CHART, click anywhere inside the Chart, then click **DESIGN TAB**, then **Change Chart Type**

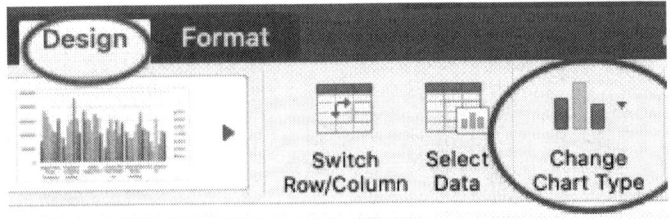

Then, select Line Chart and 2-D Line

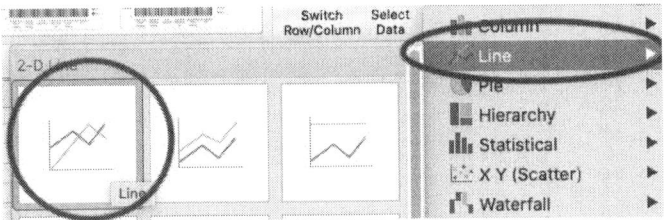

That's it! There you have your Line Chart!

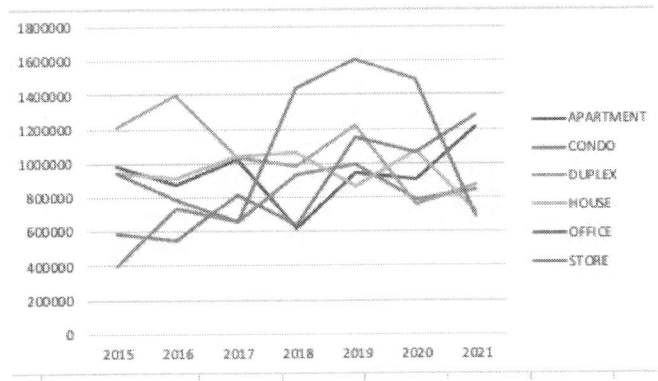

DO YOU WANT A PIE CHART? Same process, but select Pie Chart instead of

Line.

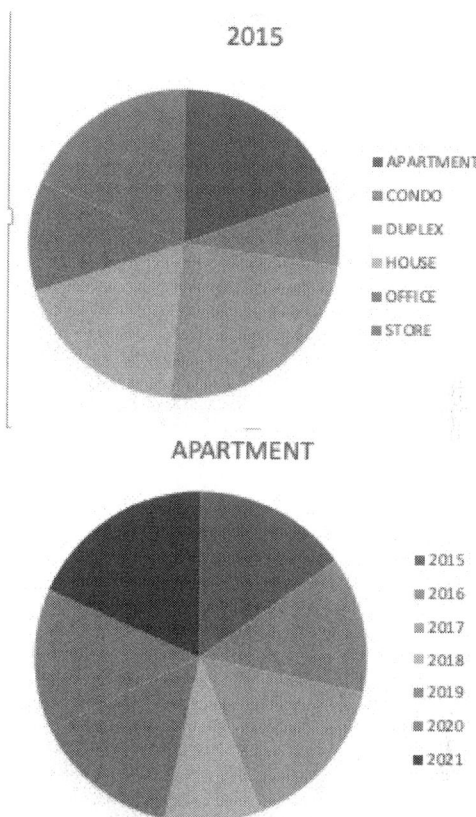

The trick with Pie charts is that you can get just 1 Type or property with all the years, OR 1 Year with all the properties.

SUPER MEGA IMPORTANT NOTE!

In the next chapter, you are going to learn how to control and manipulate your Pivot Charts to make them flexible! And it is no secret that we are going to be using SLICERS!

CONGRATULATIONS! Now you know how to create Pivot Charts, let's move to the last Chapter of this book!

MORE EXERCISES:

- PivotNinjaChapter9ex3.xlsx
- PivotNinjaChapter9ex4.xlsx

QUICK CHAPTER SUMMARY:

- Pivot Chats are flexible enough to manipulate them with a few clicks
- You can change the Row/Column section of the Chart (and the Pivot Table) with a single click

- The Pivot Charts that are most commonly used are Bar, Line and Pie, so we are going to stick to them.

CHAPTER 10

DYNAMIC PIVOT CHARTS USING SLICERS

This is the last chapter of the book. Here, you are going to combine everything you have learned throughout the book and you will find that you have developed a great set of skills.

Basically, within this chapter you are going to create a Pivot Table, then a Pivot Chart, then reorganize that Pivot Chart with the Row/Column layout that better serves you and finally you are going to insert some slicers to control the data and the Pivot Chart.

Let's start with the same 1st exercise of the previous Chapter, and let's pick it up where we left.

Open file PivotNinjaChapter10ex1.xlsx

Your job in this exercise was to create the

following Pivot Table

Create a Pivot Table that shows the Total amount Paid by each Company each Year

Then, create a Pivot Chart with it

STEP 1: Please, follow the instructions in the previous Chapter to create the Pivot Chart.

STEP 2: Please use **Switch Row/Columns** to have the Years in the X Axis (Columns) like this

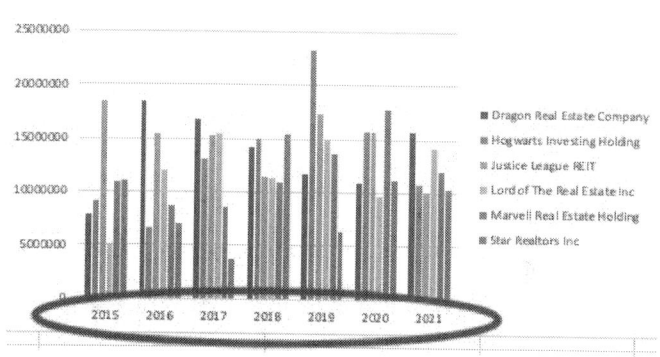

STEP 3: Now, follow the process to Create SLICERS! Click inside the Pivot Table, go to PivotTable Analyze, Insert Slicer and then insert 3 Slicers:

- YEAR
- BUYER
- CATEGORY

STEP 4: Look how awesome this is! Let's say I just want to visualize Dragon Real Estate vs Hogwarts Investing Holding.

Using the same controls as you learned in the Slicers chapter, **just select Dragon Real Estate Company and Hogwarts Investing Holding!**

EXCEL PIVOT TABLES AND PIVOT CHARTS NINJA

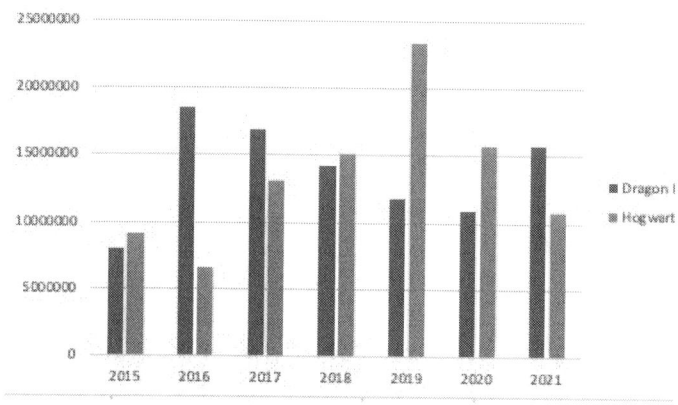

Look how the Pivot Chart was modified instantly! Just showing Dragon Real Estate vs Hogwarts Investing. This is a decluttered nice little chart!

STEP 5: Let's take this further and let's say I just want to see Dragon Real Estate vs Hogwarts Investing Holding **from 2015 to 2018.**

Just select from 2015 to 2018 in the Year Slicer and voila!

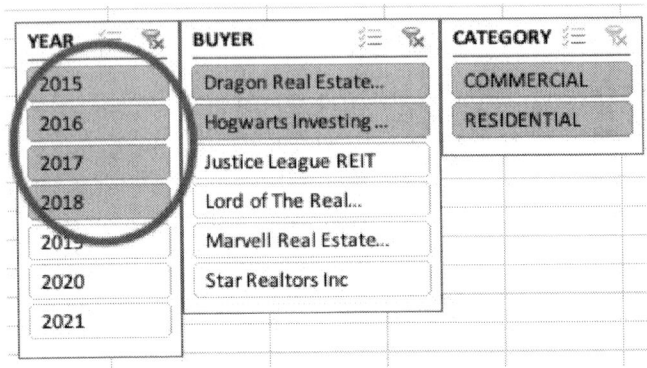

Now, you are just watching those 4 years!

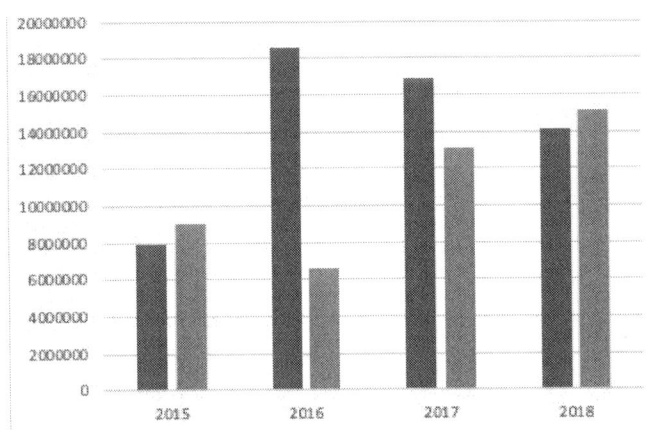

STEP 6: Let's take this further and let's say I just want to see the **COMMERCIAL PROPERTY** bought by Dragon Real Estate

vs Hogwarts Investing Holding from 2015 to 2018.

Just select from Commercial in the Category Slicer and that's it!

Now, **you are watching the Commercial Property bought by those 2 companies during 2015, 2016, 2017 and 2018.**

If you take a closer look, you'll notice that Hogwarts didn't buy any commercial property during 2016.

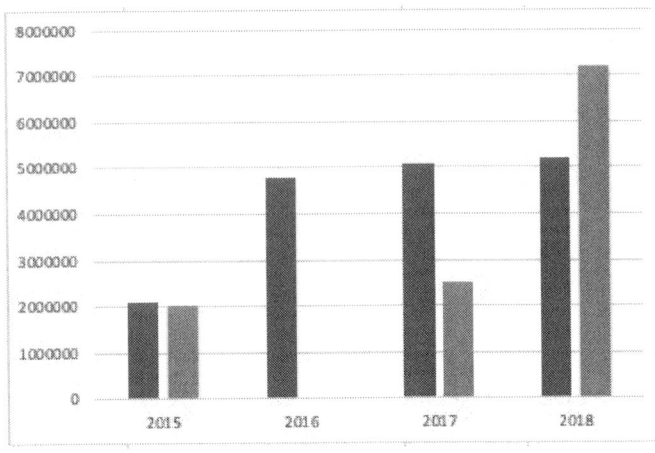

Now, let's look at the last guided exercise in the book. The Pie Pivot Chart (because this one is a little tricky)

Open file PivotNinjaChapter10ex2.xlsx

Your job in this exercise is to create the following Pivot Table

Create a Pivot Table that shows the Total Cashflow created by each Type each Year

Then, create a PIE Pivot Chart with it

STEP 1: Please, follow the instructions in the

previous Chapter to create the Pivot Chart. **(Put the YEARS into the Columns and the TYPE into the Rows)**

STEP 2: Create a PIE Pivot Chart. (Follow instructions in previous chapters to Change the kind of Chart because the first chart you are going to get is a Bar Chart)

STEP 3: Create 3 Slicers

- YEAR
- TYPE
- ZONE

You'll end up with this Pivot Table, Pivot Chart and these Slicers

Sum of YEARLY CASHFLOW	Column Labels				
Row Labels	2015	2016	2017	2018	20
APARTMENT	980229	870173	1018569	616264	9476
CONDO	398128	737799	652579	935346	9893
DUPLEX	1209966	1398331	1028740	979990	12179
HOUSE	947375	909141	1042413	1063774	8638
OFFICE	583113	544078	819121	637592	11476
STORE	940742	786951	654296	1439810	16094
Grand Total	5059552	5246473	5215719	5672777	67758

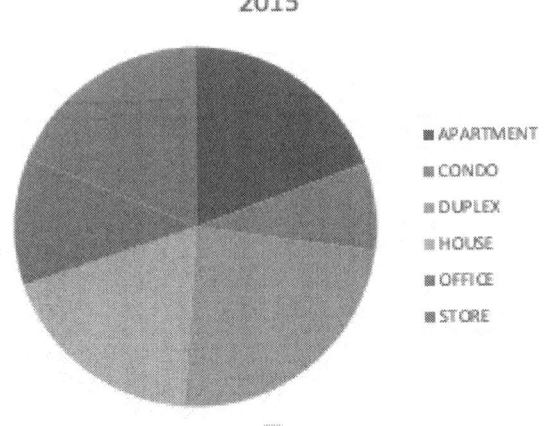

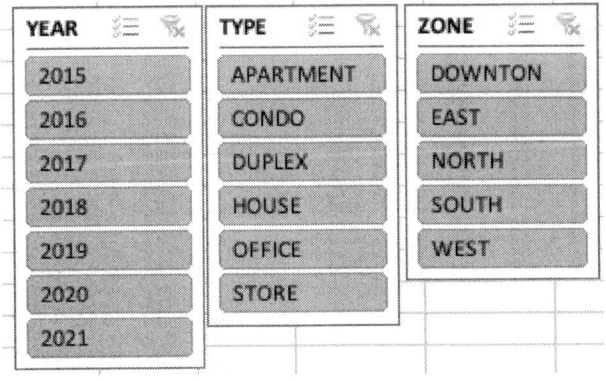

NOTE: The trick with **PIE PIVOT CHARTS** is that they are just allowed to show 1 **OF THE COLUMNS AT THE SAME TIME!** So, because **YEARS** is in you Pivot Table Columns, you are just allowed to show 1 year at a time in your Pivot Table.

Try it by selecting 2018 and 2019 in your YEAR Slicer

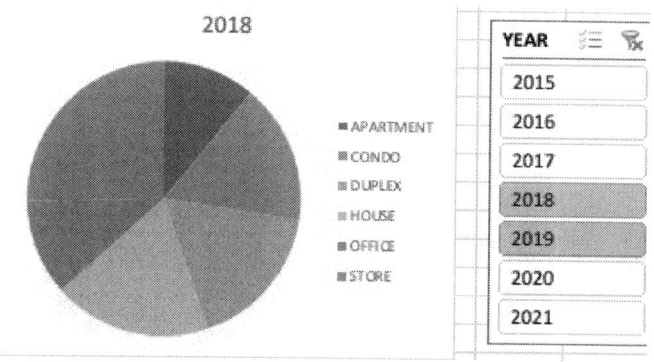

Look how the Pivot Chart just shows 2018

STEP 4: If you want to show 1 TYPE at time (instead of 1 year at a time) you need to Switch Row/Columns. Go ahead and do it.

Sum of YEARLY CASHFLOW	Column Labels				
Row Labels	APARTMENT	CONDO	DUPLEX	HOUSE	OFFI(
2018	616264	935346	979990	1063774	637
2019	947600	989318	1217974	863898	1147
Grand Total	1563865	1924664	2197964	1927672	1785

NOTE: Notice how, because you switched Rows/Columns AND you still have your Slicer filter activated (2018 and 2019) The Pivot Table just shows 2018 and 2019, and just Apartments (which is the first column now)

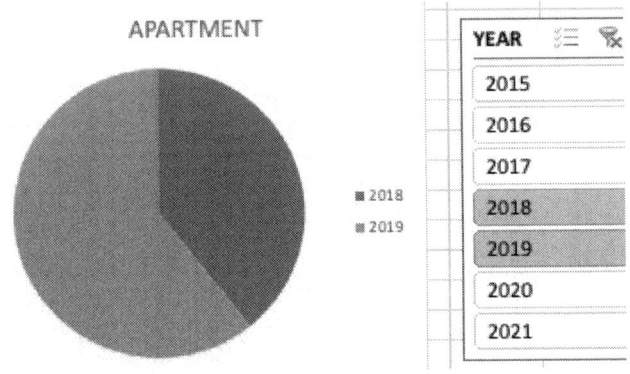

What if you want to show Cashflow generated by HOUSES throughout all the years? Just use your Slicers!

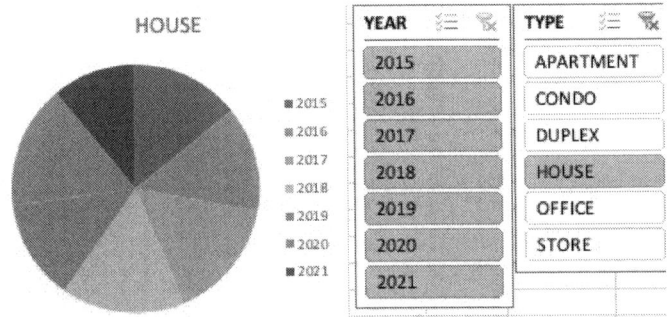

What if you want to show Cashflow generated by **OFFICES** from years 2015 to 2018 in the <u>**DOWNTOWN ZONE**</u>? Just use your Slicers!

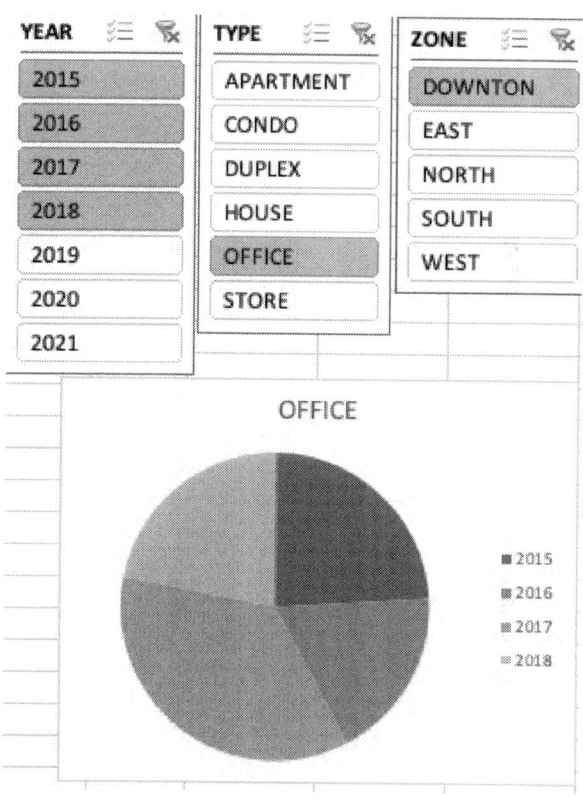

STEP 5: Do you want to embellish you Charts? Just Click on the Pivot Chart, go to DESING Tab and choose your style!

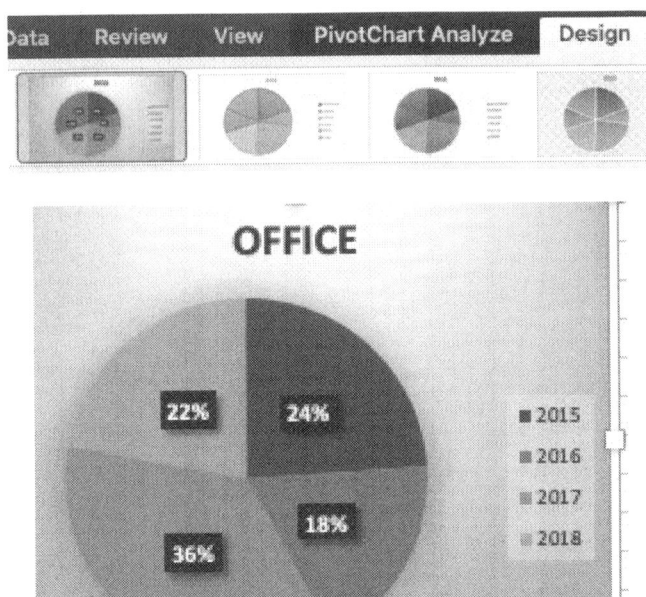

NOW THAT YOU ALREADY HAVE THE NECESSARY SKILLS, LET'S SEE WHAT YOU ARE MADE OF.

QUEST:

YOU HAVE A WHOLE LOT OF EXERCISES TO SOLVE ON YOU OWN TO COMPLETE THIS CHAPTER. WHEN YOU ARE DONE,

YOU CAN CALL YOURSELF A PIVOT TABLE AND PIVOT CHART NINJA!

I will be so happy to receive an email from you, saying that you completed all the exercises!

MORE EXERCISES:

- PivotNinjaChapter10ex3.xlsx
- PivotNinjaChapter10ex4.xlsx
- PivotNinjaChapter10ex5.xlsx
- PivotNinjaChapter10ex6.xlsx
- PivotNinjaChapter10ex7.xlsx
- PivotNinjaChapter10ex8.xlsx
- PivotNinjaChapter10ex9.xlsx
- PivotNinjaChapter10ex10.xlsx

QUICK CHAPTER SUMMARY:

- Remember to Switch Row/Column when needed
- Remember to Add Slicers as you need them

- Remember to CLEAR Slicer Filters when you don't need them anymore
- SLICERS ARE JUST AWESOME!
- Pivot Charts are the ultimate tool to convey information in depth and instantaneously!

I really enjoyed being with you all this time, and I really hope you got a great amount of value from this book. If that's the case, consider writing a review for this book where you bought it.

CHAPTER 11

QUICK FINAL TIPS

CONGRATULATIONS!! You finished the exercises and now you are an EXCEL PIVOT TABLES AND PIVOT CHARTS! It was a great journey.

This book wouldn't be complete without a series of final recommendations that can help you even more

Here (in this short chapter) I can't teach you everything I'm going to recommend because they are extensive topics that would not fit in a few pages, it is also information that I teach deeply in other Excel books.

However, I want to make the following recommendations you with the hope that you recognize the main tools that you must learn to be an EXCEL NINJA.

WHY DO YOU NEED TO LEARN MORE FUNCTIONS?

There are hundreds of functions that can help you to better perform your work, however you may not know them. Sometimes a new function that you learn can save you hours of weekly work in the office.

The important thing to remember about functions is that they tend to relate to each other and become stronger tools when combined or in the form of nested formulas.

I'll give you an example you already know: VLOOKUP. The VLOOKUP function is quite strong and useful on its own, but when you learned to use IF together with VLOOKUP, three things happened:

1) You learned a new function: VLOOKUP

2) You learned a new function: IF

3) You learned a new tool: IF + VLOOKUP

When you learn just two functions you actually have three tools in your toolbox. That is, your tools are not just the number of functions you master, but also include the combinations you can make between those functions.

So, the more functions you know, the more combinations you can make and the more chances you have to become an Excel Champion.

That is why I created Excel Formulas Ninja! The purpose of Formulas Ninja is to teach you the TOP Formulas in Excel in an Easy and Fast Way!

Get your copy of Excel Formulas Ninja here!

"A STRAIGHTFORWARD, EXERCISE-BASED AND FAST WAY TO LEARN EXCEL FUNCTIONS" - Employee from a State Department of Education

"The book was engaging and encouraging by providing many examples and exercises. I will eagerly study the other

books in the series."

WHY DO YOU NEED TO LEARN KEYBOARD SHORTCUTS?

First of all, I want to recommend that you learn Excel keyboard shortcuts. Keyboard shortcuts are the easiest and fastest way to increase your productivity in Excel. You can easily cut your work time in half.

The reality is that there are more than 100 keyboard shortcuts. My recommendation is that you learn the 10 or 20 main ones. Which are the main ones? The ones you use the most depending the kind of work you have to do in Excel.

Some of those that everybody should use are:

Ctrl + C to copy a cell (with format too)

Ctrl + V to paste the cell that you copied

Ctrl + X to cut the cell (instead of copying it, you remove it from its cell to paste it in

another cell)

Ctrl + to insert a column or row (selecting the column or row previously)

Ctrl - to delete a column or row (selecting the column or row previously)

Surely with these shortcuts you can move a little faster. But there are more that are quite useful.

"I WAS ABLE TO SAVE COUNTLESS HOURS THANKS TO THIS BOOK!"- Department Store Manager

WHY DO YOU NEED TO LEARN

CONDITIONAL FORMATTING?

You will agree that the human eye identifies faster the colors and shapes than numbers. For the same reason, traffic lights have colors instead of numbers or words.

The conditional formatting in Excel is used to add colors or shapes when certain conditions are met, making the data user-friendly and giving the opportunity to recognize patterns within the data.

Imagine for a moment that you have a table with 100 data and you need to find the values that are closest to the average.

Option 1: The first option is to use the AVERAGE function and then manually search for those values within the table.

Option 2: The fastest and easiest option is to use Conditional Format so that Excel automatically colors the data that is closest to the average, and that's it, you'll have the data you need highlighted in the color you want in a few seconds, it doesn't matter if your table has 100, 1000 or 10000 numbers.

If you would like to search for the 10 highest values within a table, you can do so. If you would like to focus only on data that is less than the average, you can color them automatically. If you want to identify the data that are between 2 values, you can do it in less than 30 seconds.

That is why I recommend conditional formatting. Becoming a Conditional Formatting Champion will allow you to find the most relevant information.

Get your copy of Conditional Formatting Champion here!

"THIS GREAT AND EASY TO

UNDERSTAND BOOK TEACHES A VERY USEFUL WAY TO ANALYZE DATA" - Accounting Manager of a Sportswear Company

WHY DO YOU NEED TO LEARN TO USE CHARTS AND DASHBOARDS?

Charts are, by excellence, the way to communicate quantitative information in the business world, in non-profit organizations, in schools, in governmental organizations, in health areas, in sports, etc.

It's very simple, if you want to effectively communicate your numerical data, you need to master the Excel Charts. That includes the use of tables and the correct positioning of them, the selection of the data that you need, the Chart Type selection and the modification of the parameters of the chart.

Additionally, it becomes necessary that you learn to discover what a chart wants to "tell you". Correctly analyzing the data in a chart usually leads to better decisions.

If you want to make better decisions in your job or company, it is very likely that becoming an Excel Charts and Graphs Champion will benefit you

I WOULD LOVE TO READ YOUR COMMENTS

Before you go, I would like to tell you Thank You for buying my book. It is my wish that the information you obtained in **EXCEL PIVOT TABLES AND PIVOT CHARTS NINJA** helps you in your job or business, and that you can have greater productivity and more free time to use it in the activities that you like the most.

I realize that you could have chosen among several other Excel books but you chose **EXCEL PIVOT TABLES AND PIVOT CHARTS NINJA** and you invested your time and effort. I am honored to have the opportunity to help you.

I'd like to ask you a small favor. <u>**Could you take a minute or two and leave a Review of EXCEL PIVOT TABLES AND PIVOT CHARTS NINJA on Amazon?**</u>

This feedback will be very appreciated and will help me continue to write more courses that help you and a lot more people.

Share your comments with me and other readers

ABOUT THE AUTHOR

Henry E. Mejia is passionate about progress and goal achieving, he also loves to run and exercise. He works in the insurance industry and likes to invest in the stock market. While doing that, he devotes some time to create Excel written courses like this one, in order to help people to achieve their professional goals.

Henry also realized that the vast majority of people use a lot of their work time in front of the computer. That time could be used in more productive or more enjoyable activities, only if people knew how to use Excel a little better.

The goal of Henry's books is to open the door for workers and business owners to use Excel more efficiently, so they can have more and better growth opportunities, progress and free time.

Printed in Great Britain
by Amazon